TOP
OF THE
CITY

NEW YORK'S HIDDEN
ROOFTOP WORLD

LAURA ROSEN

Thames and Hudson

For my parents

First published in the United States by Thames and Hudson Inc.,
500 Fifth Avenue, New York, New York 10110
Reprinted 1990
First published in Great Britain in 1982 by Thames and Hudson Ltd, London
Reprinted 1990

Library of Congress Catalog Card Number 82-80589
ISBN: 0-500-01288-1
0-500-27269-7 (paperback)

Designed by Janet Doyle

Printed in Japan by Dai Nippon

CONTENTS

Foreword by Brendan Gill

Introduction

Chapter I: Commercial Heights and Civic Towers

Chapter II: Residential High Country

Chapter III: The Decorated Roofscape

Chapter IV: A Skyline Miscellany

Acknowledgments

This book would not have been possible without the help of many people who generously gave me access to their terraces, roofs and windows. I owe special gratitude to Margaret R. Weiss, Judith Litchfield, and the New York Department of Buildings. Finally, I wish to thank Dudley Witney for his limitless encouragement, advice and patience.

Books that were especially helpful in my research include *The City Observed: New York* (Vintage Books) and *The Skyscraper* (Alfred H. Knopf) by Paul Goldberger; *AIA Guide to New York City* edited by Norval White and Elliot Willensky (Macmillan); and *Skyscraper Style* by Cervin Robinson and Rosemarie Haag Bletter (Oxford University Press).

I drew upon the extensive files of the New York Department of Buildings, as well as the books I have mentioned, for the historical and architectural documentation presented here. Occasionally, these sources disagree and sometimes there is no information at all about certain buildings. I have also been aided by the recollections of individuals.

Foreword

Within living memory, the usual approach to New York was by ship. Standing on deck, the traveler would find his eye drawn insistently upward from a smudged pencil-line of piers and wharves to that cluster of bright pinnacles which, rising in romantic disorder from the water's edge, stamped a not at all reticent message in bold strokes against the sky. "Behold us, wonders of the New World!" they seemed to say. "Measure if you can the energy and ambition that have made us possible!" To this day, whether afloat or ashore, the eye continues to seek instruction and delight hundreds of feet above our soiled and littered pavements. We look up, knowing that it is upon the tops of buildings that, generation after generation, the architects of the city have lavished their talents; it is there that they have given their so often hobbled imaginations full rein. In the late nineteenth century, the tops of skyscrapers often took the shape of domes, surmounted by jaunty gilded lanterns; later came ziggurats, mausoleums, Alexandrian lighthouses, miniature Parthenons. These charm-

7

ing follies contained neither royal corpses nor effigies of gods and goddesses; rather, they contained large wooden tanks filled with water. Though to the stroller in the street such a folly would appear to have no purpose other than that of completing the design of a building in an artistic fashion, it is, in fact, part of the indispensable mechanical guts of the building.

By universal consent, the classic skyscraper form is that of the Woolworth Building, completed in 1913 to the designs of Cass Gilbert. Its steel frame clad in flamboyant Gothic tracery, complete even to gargoyles, it was at once nicknamed "the cathedral of commerce." Not that any divinity ever worshiped there; the building was erected by Mammon to celebrate Mammon, its owner, Frank Woolworth, having made his fortune by the founding of a chain of five-and-ten-cent stores throughout the country. For many years it was the tallest inhabited structure on earth (the Eiffel Tower, in Paris, was the highest uninhabited structure); it was said to have cost thirteen million dollars, which Mr. Woolworth handed over in cold cash—one would like to think, in nickels and dimes. In the 1980s, the Woolworth Building was admirably restored, at something like one and a half times its original cost.

Two other celebrated New York skyscrapers designed during the first third of the twentieth century are the Chrysler Building and the Empire State Building. They are both true towers, though if the Empire State Building had not affixed to its flat top a never-to-be-used mast for the mooring of dirigibles and to that mast had not subsequently affixed a still higher mast for the transmitting of radio and television programs, it would have revealed itself to be in the vanguard of a new generation of skyscrapers, severely cubical in elevation, which after the Second World War developed into the sleek, non-expressive slab—"high-rises," as they came to be called, and rightly so, for while they nudged the sky, or perhaps even attempted to shoulder it aside, they gave no sense of aspiring to scrape it. In the era of the slab, there was no occasion for finial follies: water tanks, like air-conditioning equipment and the other increasingly complex mechanical requirements of a high-rise, were housed within its undifferentiated envelope. Only now, in the 1980s, has the tower begun to make an unexpected comeback. So far, the most spectacular example is the A.T.&T. tower, designed by Philip Johnson and John Burgee, which at first glance looks as if it might be the ghost of some turn-of-the-century Wall Street structure that, losing its way after long absence (as even ghosts will), has stumbled unwittingly onto Madison Avenue, in the heart of midtown. At a second glance, one perceives how subtly the exaggerations of scale in the A.T.&T. Building pay homage to classical predecessors without imitating them—the homage is authentic and yet playful, a salute by youth to age, by the present to the past.

To speak of ghosts is to call attention to one of the major challenges that any photographer of New York City must confront and overcome. We are a city notorious for our wasteful, exuberant practice of constantly knocking down and building up, knocking down and building up, and the ill-matched fabric of diverse materials that is a consequence of this practice requires a close reading. The visible city is the photographer's subject, but concealed behind its myriad facades are those anonymous generations who first lifted the facades into place;

they, too, deserve to be recognized and, in some fashion, to have their likenesses taken. For the population of a city consists not only of its current inhabitants but also of the ghosts of its builders. Occupying no space, casting no shadows, they yet charge the air with precious clues, both sad and joyous. The lilt of felt life that a Laura Rosen in her enthusiasm and talent discovers, whether on an obscure, tar-papered rooftop or in the delectable curve of some sooty limestone modillion, is truly discovered and not imposed; it bears witness to a human presence that the young may be better able to detect and celebrate than we older residents of the city, on whom familiarity has bestowed a certain cautionary blindness. In New York, the dulling of the senses is commonly thought to help keep us sane; we see, hear, touch, taste, and smell much less than we might, on the silently consented-to premise that the full impact of our incomparable city—raw, passionate, importunate, unfinished, unfinishable—might be more than we could bear. Rosen fears no such burdens; however heavy they might strike us as being, they are light to her, and she pursues them sometimes (I am thinking of the acrobatic postures that she has had to assume at great heights in order to obtain a number of the pictures in this book) almost literally at the risk of her life.

There are writers to whom nothing can be said to have happened until after they have succeeded in setting it down in words. In a not dissimilar fashion, there are photographers for whom the rendering is the reality—to the degree to which it can be claimed to exist at all, the thing-in-itself is but a necessary means to an end: an image on a piece of paper. Rosen is not that kind of photographer. Her subject-matter is always of itself and complete in itself, but the zest of the taker of the picture is also present; little by little as we study her pictures we make acquaintance with her quiddity. Plainly, she is (as I am) a devoted amateur of architectural history; plainly, she has (as I wish I had) a sharp eye for the bizarre, mingled with tenderness. Here is a plump cherub, carved above the entrance to a shabby, once-grand hotel in the West Thirties; here, too, are Louis Sullivan's angels, benignly brooding above the dirt and clamor of Bleecker Street. How many creatures Rosen has befriended! Lions and bears have posed for her with the passive tranquillity of lambs, and so have rabbits, eagles, and salamanders, to say nothing of caryatids, robustly topless in dress, and many a smiling saint.

The nature of New York, like the nature of any great city (one thinks of Venice), remains in large part mysterious. We who have lived here all our lives must confess at last that we love a city that we have never wholly known. As we grow older, the mystery appears to deepen rather than diminish; marching towards the heart of the mystery, we feel surrounded by a not unfriendly darkness. Rosen's city—the city of the sky—is filled with nourishing light, but there are hints here and there throughout this book that she is mindful of the fact that high buildings cast shadows: that the life of a street in shadow is silver as well as gray and furnishes its own singular forms of nourishment. No doubt some day she and her camera will address that city as well, making all the rest of us, then as now, the beneficiaries of her arduous and exquisite vocation.

Brendan Gill

Introduction

In the 1950s, when I was growing up, New York was the most populous city in the world, and its famous skyline consisted of the tallest buildings in the world. I lived in a New Jersey suburb, but Manhattan was where my father worked, where my mother went to find special things for the house, and where we all went to visit museums and see Broadway shows and eat in wonderful restaurants. New York was where things were bigger and better than anywhere else.

A trip to the city was a special event for me and I usually wore white gloves and a dress. I felt a certain pride when I looked up at the Empire State Building and the Chrysler Building because I knew that there were no taller buildings anywhere. The tall buildings transformed the streets and avenues into great canyons, striped with the skyscrapers' long black shadows. When I was old enough to notice other cities, I was struck by the absence of tall buildings. I had thought that skyscrapers were what physically defined a city, and I was surprised when other cities appeared to be only vast stretches of outskirts.

I had always wanted to live and work in Manhattan and I moved there after college. New York was no longer the world's most populous city with the world's tallest buildings, but it was still the ultimate skyscraper city, as awe-inspiring as ever. Within a couple of years, I was working as an architectural photographer, documenting buildings for architects, museums and publications.

My clients' requirements were extremely varied. Sometimes I was asked to document an historical building, showing every aspect of its design, condition and surroundings so that a curator or restoration architect could refer to the photographs when it was not possible to be at the building itself. Other times, architects wanted photographs that would isolate and dramatize their buildings. I shot a new office tower in midtown, for example, from a tenth-floor setback of a neighboring building, from which vantage point no other building blocked or upstaged the architect's creation, and no signs, street lights or traffic detracted from the building. A polarizing filter made the building brighter and the sky bluer. The end product was an image of a pristine, sparkling object untouched by its environment.

I spent a lot of time on the tops of buildings doing these assignments, and I became aware of a different, alluring reality created by Manhattan's rooftops. There is a mysterious thrill to

being on the roof of a tall building. On the street, one's surroundings are identified by familiar entrances, signs and locations on the street grid. Up high, the familiar context vanishes. Tar paper becomes the ground from which towers, temples, cornices, chimneys and water tanks dramatically rise. The city is transformed from a place of crowded canyon streets into an environment of fantasy structures and illusive scale. Towers that I had noticed many times before turned out to be the tops of buildings whose entrances I knew. Unpretentious apartment houses revealed elaborate penthouses and roof gardens. Gargoyles I never knew existed were at my feet. To the eye, this world appears to be empty, but the mind knows it is full of people. On my own, I began to photograph this unknown environment that exists above the familiar one.

Gaining access to roofs, terraces and upper story windows was part of the challenge of this exploration. Office building windows were the most readily available vantage points. Many of the photographs were taken from windows I had chosen from street level because they appeared to have desirable views. I would count the number of floors up to the window and go in and ask people on that floor if I could use one of their office windows to take a photograph for my book. They almost always said yes. People usually were curious about the project and showed me their favorite parts of the view. Sometimes they brought me a cup of coffee and a doughnut and asked what kind of camera I thought they should buy. Some people even showed me their own pictures of the view. I barged into all kinds of business establishments, from television producers' offices to sweat shops to Indian importers' warehouses to photo studios. I found a lot of enthusiasm for the concept of the book as I made my rounds.

Although commercial tenants were usually cooperative, managing agents of buildings frequently were not, making it necessary to sneak up to certain roofs. Buildings that were both owned and managed by the same corporation were far more likely to let me photograph from their roofs; Rockefeller Center, Metropolitan Life, Sage Realty and AT&T were among those that gave me permission. Each is a proud empire with employees who give their buildings affectionate care and who like to show them off; they generally supplied me with security escorts as well as someone who could answer my questions about the building.

At first, residential buildings seemed inaccessible. People are far more likely to let a stranger into their offices than their homes. I began by asking everyone I met if he or she knew of any apartments with a good view or an interesting roof or terrace. Eventually this created a network of "informants," and people started letting me know when they discovered new vantage points.

The roofscape has become a special frontier for me, existing above my well-mapped city life. The photographs in this book, all taken in Manhattan, are the result of my exploration of that frontier over a period of three years. It was an exploration done out of love for the city.

Commercial Heights and Civic Towers

Manhattan is the city of the famous skyline. The World and Tribune buildings, considered by some architectural historians to have been the world's first skyscrapers, went up in 1875. From that time until the Great Depression of the 1930s, large corporations competed to build the tallest, most distinctive buildings in the skyline, topping their skyscrapers with fanciful temples, obelisks and statues. The grand finale was the Empire State Building, completed

continued

in 1931, which was topped with an airship mooring that was never used.

In more recent times, intensive construction in the International Style has turned parts of the skyline into skyclumps, especially in midtown. Nondescript boxes have replaced many older buildings, filling the spaces between the survivors and making it hard to pick out individual structures—the new buildings are difficult to tell apart and the old ones are hidden behind them. Wall Street had become a skyclump before the International Style arrived, but the gigantic old buildings, many of which are still intact, are so flamboyant that they still insist upon attention. 70 Pine Street, the former Cities Service Building, has a stone model of itself at its entrance to make sure that passersby know which skyscraper it is.

There has been a recent revival of interest in the tops of skyscrapers. Dramatic new night lighting enlivens the tops of the Helmsley, Chrysler, Metropolitan Life, Empire State and Con Edison buildings. One Astor Plaza, the Citicorp Center and the AT&T Building are among several new buildings designed with unusual rooflines. As interesting as the shapes of these new rooftops are, they don't look like idyllic or amusing places to be. A slide down Citicorp's roof is a terrifying thought.

1

26 Broadway, originally the Standard Oil Building. Architects: Carrère & Hastings; Shreve, Lamb & Blake. 1926. The building's tower is seen against New York Harbor. The Statue of Liberty is at upper right.

2

The former United States
Custom House at
Bowling Green.
Architect: Cass Gilbert.
1907.
The tower visible above
the old Custom House is
26 Broadway.

3

3

90 West Street.
Architect: Cass Gilbert.
1905.
The World Trade Center
towers form the striped
backdrop.

4
The Bankers Trust
Building at 16 Wall
Street.
Architects: Trowbridge
& Livingston. 1912.
This pyramid is a
corporate symbol for
Bankers Trust.

5
The Criminal Courts
Building and Prison, also
known as "The Tombs,"
at 100 Centre Street.
Architects: Harvey Wiley
Corbett and Charles B.
Meyers. 1939.

6
City Hall at City Hall
Park.
Architects: Joseph F.
Mangin and John
McComb, Jr. 1811.
The Criminal Court of
the City of New York,

also known as the
"Tweed Courthouse."
Architect: John Kellum.
1872.
Justice holds her scales
over City Hall with her
back to the skylights of
the Tweed Courthouse.

5

6

7

The three towers are, from left to right, the United States Courthouse, the Municipal Building and the Park Row Building.
The United States Courthouse at Foley Square.
Architects: Cass Gilbert and Cass Gilbert, Jr. 1936.
The Municipal Building at Chambers and Centre Streets.
Architects: McKim, Mead & White. 1914.
The Park Row Building at 15 Park Row.
Architect: Robert H. Robertson. 1899.

8

The Royal Insurance
Company Building at
150 William Street.
Architects: Starrett &
Van Vleck. 1931.
The penthouse was
originally the
superintendent's
apartment; today it is
storage space for
maintenance equipment.

9

*24 Water Street.
This building belongs to
the Sons of the American
Revolution. Behind it is
the ITT Building at 67
Broad Street, designed by
Buchman & Kahn and
completed in 1929.*

10

*70 Pine Street. The
American International
Building.
Architects: Clinton &
Russell. 1932.
Originally the Cities
Service building at 60
Wall Street. Cities
Service wanted their Pine
Street building to have a
Wall Street address, so a
footbridge was built to
connect the giant tower
to a small building on
Wall Street a block away.
In the late seventies,
Cities Service left New
York and the Wall Street
building and bridge were
demolished when the
tower was sold. The new
owners constructed a
new bridge, this one to
72 Wall Street, but have
accepted a Pine Street
address.*

11

1181 Broadway. The Baudouine Building. Architect: Alfred Zucker. 1896.

12

1170 Broadway.
Architects: DeLemos &
Cordes. c. 1903.
These buildings face
each other at 28th Street
and Broadway.

14

13

The Candler Building at 220 West 42nd Street. 1912.

14

The New York Times Building at 229 West 43rd Street. Architects: Ludlow & Peabody. 1923.

15

The American–Standard
Building. Originally the
American Radiator
Building at 40 West 40th
Street.
Architects: Hood &
Fouilhoux. 1924.

16

1384 Broadway.
Formerly the Lefcourt
Normandie Building.
Architects: Bark &
Djorup. 1928.

17

295 Madison Avenue.
Architects: Attributed to
both Bark & Djorup and
Charles F. Moyer
Company. 1929, 1930.

18

170 Fifth Avenue.
Architect: Robert
Maynicke. 1898.
Maynicke wrote on his
plan application that this
galvanized-iron tower
was to be used
specifically as an artist's
studio and not for
storage. The Flatiron
Building is to the left.

19

331 Madison Avenue.
Architect: Attributed to
both H. Craig Severance
and Charles I. Berg.
1911.
The Chrysler Building is
in the background.

18

The World's Tallest Buildings

Frank Woolworth, owner of the five-and-ten-cent stores, paid thirteen million dollars in cash to build his 792-foot skyscraper, which was the tallest office building in the world until the Chrysler Building surpassed it in 1931. The F.W. Woolworth Co. still owns the building and has recently given it a twenty-million-dollar restoration. Much of the original terra-cotta ornamentation had to be removed from the top of the building because it had seriously decayed. Now, simpler aluminum and fiberglass forms replace the terra-cotta buttresses, gargoyles and tourelles.

Walter Chrysler wanted the world's tallest building, and there were a number of stories at the time about the way he achieved his wish. According to one story, when his building was nearing completion, the Bank of the Manhattan Company's tower finished construction at

20

The Woolworth Building at 233 Broadway. Architect: Cass Gilbert. 1913.

927 feet, two feet higher than the Chrysler Building's dome. Chrysler had his architect, William Van Alen, secretly design a spire to be constructed inside the dome and then lifted through it to bring the building's height to 1,048 feet. This would also be a victory for Van Alen because the architect of the other building, H. Craig Severance, was his former partner. Another story had it that the spire was part of the original design and that Chrysler was actually competing with the North Building of the Metropolitan Life Insurance Company for which drawings had been published showing a proposed record-breaking height. But when the building was completed, it only reached 28 stories. The Chrysler Building was the first structure to surpass the Eiffel Tower's 984-foot record. The year after it was completed it lost the world's record to the Empire State Building.

21

The Chrysler Building at 405 Lexington Avenue. Architect: William Van Alen. 1930.

22

*North Building of the
Metropolitan Life
Insurance Company, at
25 Madison Avenue.
Architects: Harvey Wiley
Corbett and D. Everett
Waid. 1932.*

23

40 Wall Street. Originally the Bank of the Manhattan Company Building.
Architects: H. Craig Severance and Yasuo Matsui, 1929.

24

25

24, 25, 26, and 27

The Empire State Building at 350 Fifth Avenue.
Architects: Shreve, Lamb & Harmon. 1931.
The Empire State Building is visible above the tops of buildings all over midtown.
In addition, the Park Row Building (#44 in the color section) was also the tallest building in its day.

26

27

28 and 29

Office buildings on Avenue of the Americas. The three similar buildings with narrow vertical stripes are the Celanese Building, the McGraw-Hill Building and the Exxon Building, all part of the Rockefeller Center extension designed by Harrison & Abramovitz & Harris and built in the early seventies. In the other photograph, joggers are seen on the McGraw-Hill Building roof.

30

1501 Broadway.
Originally the
Paramount Building.
Architects: Rapp &
Rapp. 1927.
One Astor Plaza.
Architects: Kahn &
Jacobs. 1969.
Both of these buildings
face Times Square.

31

New York Telephone Company Building at 375 Pearl Street. Architects: Rose, Beaton & Rose. 1975.

43

32 and 33

*The World Trade Center
between Church, Vesey,
West and Liberty Streets.
Architects: Minoru
Yamasaki & Associates;
Emery Roth & Sons.
1970–77.
The visitor is looking
down over the landfill for
Battery Park City.*

34

27–29 West 57th Street. Originally the American Piano Company Building. Architects: Cross & Cross. 1924. The Solow Building at

9 West 57th Street. Architects: Skidmore, Owings & Merrill. 1974. The Solow Building's curved facade sweeps by its gracious neighbor.

35

The Citicorp Center between Lexington and Third Avenues, 53rd to 54th Streets. Architects: Hugh Stubbins & Associates. 1977.

36

The AT&T Building at
550 Madison Avenue.
Architects:
Johnson/Burgee.
Projected completion:
1983.

The Roofscape in Color

37

The Bank of New York Building at 48 Wall Street.
Architect: Benjamin Wistar Morris. 1929. Behind the top of the Bank of New York's tower are seen parts of three East River bridges. The closest is the Brooklyn Bridge, the second is the Manhattan Bridge with a subway crossing it, and to the north is the Williamsburg Bridge.

38

*The Helmsley Building,
originally the New York
Central Building at 230
Park Avenue.
Architects: Warren &
Wetmore. 1929.*

39 and 40

*Metropolitan Life Tower and
clock at 1 Madison Avenue.
Architects: Napoleon
LeBrun & Sons. 1909.
The night lighting on the
tower changes for
seasons and holidays. At
Christmas it is lit like a
huge Christmas tree.*

40

39

41

*The General Electric
Building, originally the
RCA Building, at 570
Lexington Avenue.
Architects: Cross &
Cross. 1931.
The top is a crown of
stone and polychrome
with gold radio waves.*

42

*New York Life Insurance
Co. Building at 51
Madison Avenue.
Architect: Cass Gilbert.
1928.
The gold tile top is seen
from a balcony which
circles its base.*

43

Grand Central Terminal at 42nd Street and Park Avenue.
Architects: Reed & Stem; Warren & Wetmore. 1913. Sculptor of clock and surrounding ornament: Jules Coutan.

44

The Park Row Building at 15 Park Row. Architect: Robert H. Robertson. 1899. This was once the world's tallest office building.

45 and 46

The American Telephone and Telegraph Building at 195 Broadway. Architect: William Welles Bosworth. 1917. Evelyn Beatrice Longman's sculpture "The Genius of Electricity" served both as a corporate symbol and as a lightning rod. In 1930, it was renamed "The Spirit of Communication" when an illustration of the sculpture was used on the cover of the New York telephone directories. AT&T employees refer to it as "Golden Boy." In 1980, as construction began on the new AT&T headquarters at 550 Madison Avenue, a crew of art restorers surrounded the sculpture with scaffolding and removed it, piece by piece, from its pedestal. Sixty-three years of lightning-rod duties had

left "Golden Boy" in a weakened condition. After a restoration, which will include $18,000 worth of gold leaf, the statue will have a new home in the lobby of the new AT&T headquarters.

47

730 Fifth Avenue, originally the Heckscher Building. Architects: Whitney, Warren & Wetmore. 1921. The new IBM Building is under construction in the background.

48

The Fred F. French Building at 551 Fifth Avenue.
Architects: Sloan & Robertson. 1927.

49

616–32 Avenue of the Americas, originally Siegel–Cooper's Store.
Architects: DeLemos & Cordes. 1896.
Before World War I, Siegel–Cooper's was one of New York's largest and most famous stores. By 1913, it was out of business because its owners did not have the foresight to build their palatial establishment further uptown, as their successful competitors did. The corrugated iron encloses what was once a large greenhouse that contained tropical gardens open to the public. Today, the building contains commercial lofts, studios and printing companies.

Residential High Country

Although Manhattan's residential buildings don't reach the heights of the tallest commercial skyscrapers, a number of them are as exuberantly decorated, such as the Dakota, Alwyn Court, the Ansonia Hotel and the San Remo. Most other residential buildings are more discreetly embellished, mainly at the entrance and sometimes on the roof with elaborate water tank enclosures. Late in the afternoon, as the row of temples and pavilions that top the Fifth Avenue

continued
apartment buildings along Central Park catches the golden light of the setting sun, these aeries look like the most romantic homes in the world, until one realizes that most of them house water tanks or elevator machinery. A closer look reveals the much smaller pent-houses nestled at the temples' feet.

A tenant whose apartment includes a private

50

terrace or rooftop can create his own Mount Olympus by surrounding himself with gardens, trees and sculptures. People who don't have their own private rooftops or terraces can still be found on top of buildings they live in because most small apartment buildings and brownstones have easy access to the roof. In pleasant weather, figures on beach towels with books and radios dot the tarry black roofscape.

51

50

The Dakota at 1 West 72nd Street.
Architect: Henry J. Hardenbergh. 1884.
The Dakota was built as one of Manhattan's first luxury apartment buildings and has always remained fashionable.

51

The Ansonia Hotel at 2109 Broadway.
Architects: Graves & Duboy. Designer: W.E.D. Stokes. 1904.
The Ansonia has traditionally housed a great number of musicians. Singers and instrumentalists can be heard from the street and in the hallways.

The Ansonia and the Dakota are the Upper West Side's most famous residential buildings.

Apartment buildings on Fifth Avenue

52
*990 Fifth Avenue.
Architect: Rosario
Candela. 1927.*

53
1030 Fifth Avenue.
Architect: J.E.R.
Carpenter. 1925.

54

*1115 Fifth Avenue.
Architect: J.E.R.
Carpenter. 1925.*

55

*2 East 88th Street.
Architects: Pennington,
Lewis & Miller Inc.*

1040 Fifth Avenue.
Architect: Rosario
Candela. 1930.

57

*The San Remo
Apartments at 145
Central Park West.
Architect: Emery Roth.
1930.*

58

*View from the East Side
across the Central Park
reservoir toward the twin
towers of the Eldorado
Towers apartment
building at 300 Central
Park West.
Architects: Margon &
Holder. 1931.*

59

Townhouse at 42
Riverside Drive.
Architect: Charles Buck.
1897.

60

The Hendrik Hudson
apartment building at
380 Riverside Drive.
Architects: Rouse &
Sloan. 1907.

61
Riverside Drive roofs.

62

East Side apartment buildings.

63

*Terrace in Gramercy
Park district.*

64

*Roofscape in the East
Sixties.*

View from West Side roo
across Central Park
toward midtown.

66
East Side roof garden.

*Penthouse on office
building at 19–25 West
44th Street.
Architects: Starrett &
Van Vleck. c. 1917.*

68

*Penthouse on office
building at 275 Madison
Avenue.*

69

Roof in Madison Square district.

70

A clapboard cottage on top of an 1891 McKim, Mead & White office building at 907 Broadway.

71

12 East 20th Street.
Originally this was a
Lord & Taylor store.
Architect: James H.
Giles. 1869.

72
Roofs in the West Fifties.

73

73

*Washington Heights
roofs.*

74

West Side roof garden.

80

75 and 76

Sunbathers on Upper West Side.

77 and 78

Upper West Side
rooftops.

The Roofscape
in Color

82

*The Sherry Netherland
Hotel at Fifth Avenue
and 59th Street.
Architects: Schultze &
Weaver. 1927.*

83

83

Upper East Side apartment building.

85

Tudor City at East 40th Street to East 43rd Street, between First and Second Avenues. Architects: Fred F. French Company. 1928. Because the developer Fred F. French placed this middle-class residential complex in the midst of a slum and packing-house district, most of the windows of its twelve towering buildings face inward to a private park and street, with very few overlooking the surrounding area. Today, Tudor City's neighbors are elegant and include the United Nations, the Ford Foundation Building and the UN Plaza Hotel. Ironically, Harry Helmsley, the present owner of the complex, has been planning to build in the park; thus the tenants will have virtually no view at all.

84

84

*1200 Broadway, originally the Gilsey Hotel.
Architect: Stephen D. Hatch. 1869.
When new, this cast-iron building was a fashionable hotel. After it closed in 1904, however, it suffered decades of neglect as a commercial building. Recently, the building has been restored as a cooperative apartment house. During that restoration, a coat of iron oxide paint made the cast-iron exterior bright orange; today it is brown and beige. The Empire State Building is seen above it.*

86

Truck billboard seen from the West Side Highway at 40th Street. This section of the highway has since been demolished, but the billboard remains.

87

87

Fox Audubon Theater at 3940–60 Broadway. Architect: Thomas W. Lamb. 1914.

88

Statue of Liberty on the roof of the Liberty Storage Co. warehouse at 43 West 64th Street. The owners of the building say the statue was erected around 1901.

89

Surrogates Court and Hall of Records at 31 Chambers Street. Architects: John R. Thomas; Horgan Slattery. 1911.

89

90

This white stucco house in Lower Manhattan encloses elevator machinery.

91

Setback on 127 John Street.
Architects: Emery Roth & Sons. 1972.
Designer of setbacks: Pamela Waters.
Developer Melvyn Kaufman commissioned Pamela Waters, a designer, to add interest to this Lower Manhattan office building. Shown here is the east facade setback with a bird and nest. A close look at the window washer's rig reveals that it has been designed to look like a baby bird. The rig is stored on the setback when it is not moving about the building.

92

Upper West Side terrace.

93

West Village roof garden.

93

94

95

The Decorated Roofscape

The density of the city's construction makes its profusion of decorative details hard to see, but the gargoyles, goddesses and garlands that are lost to us from the streets delight and entertain us when we're up there with them.

Ironically, much rooftop embellishment has survived because of neglect. While the street levels of many older buildings have been "modernized" to attract new tenants and lure customers into their stores, the upper stories are less visible and more expensive

96

91 Fifth Avenue.
Architect: Louis Korn.
1896.

97

20 Exchange Place.
Originally the City Bank
Farmer's Trust Company
Building.
Architects: Cross &
Cross. 1931.

continued
to alter. Sometimes they are forgotten altogether until a chunk of the building comes crashing down to the sidewalk. There are whole districts which have survived in this manner. The old shopping area known as "the Ladies' Mile," between 14th Street and 23rd Street on Broadway, Fifth Avenue and Avenue of the Americas, is one such district. Here, the great retail palaces of a century ago now exist as loft buildings containing garment manufacturers, printing companies, photography studios and other businesses. Another district is around Broadway and Bleecker Streets, and SoHo is

another. In recent years, these districts have been discovered by developers who are restoring many of the buildings and converting them into luxurious co-ops.

The stone carvers who worked on Manhattan's buildings in the nineteenth and early twentieth centuries were generally Italian immigrants who worked for low wages and were regarded as common laborers, not artists. Very little is known of these individuals.

There are thriving shops around town where one can purchase a gargoyle or other piece of ornament from a demolished building to decorate a living room or garden.

98

150 Nassau Street. Originally the American Tract Society Building. Architect: Robert H. Robertson. 1895.

99

Grant's Tomb at Riverside Drive and West 122nd Street. Architect: John H. Duncan. 1897.

The Dorilton at 171 West
71st Street.
Architects: Janes & Leo.
1900.

101 and 102

The Camelot Building at 13–15 West 28th Street. Architects: Barney & Chapman. 1896. From the street one only sees the Camelot Building's decorative bands, but from a nearby roof one can see a row of caryatids below the cornice.

105

106

*The Wolcott Hotel at
4–10 West 31st Street.
Architect: John H.
Duncan. 1904.*

107

*186 Fifth Avenue.
Originally a Western
Union building.
Architect: Henry J.
Hardenbergh. 1884.*

109

108

7 St. Mark's Place.
Architect: Jobst
Hoffmann. 1890.

109

New York Stock
Exchange at 8 Broad
Street.
Architect: George B.
Post. 1903.

110

175 Fifth Avenue.
Originally the Fuller
Building. Popularly
known as the Flatiron
Building.
Architects: D.H.
Burnham & Company.
1902.
The Metropolitan Life
Tower is in the
background.

111

College Residence Hotel,
originally the Hendrik
Hudson annex, at 601
Cathedral Parkway.
Architects: Snelling &
Potter. c. 1907.

112

The Republic National
Bank, originally the
Knox Hat Building at 452
Fifth Avenue.
Architect: John H.
Duncan. 1902.

112

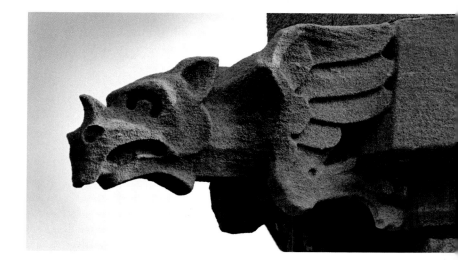

113
West Side building.

114
*2 Bennett Avenue.
Architects: Lang &
Rosenberg. 1928.*

115
*Gargoyle from
Hotel Des Artistes
at 1 West 67th
Street.
Architect: George Mort
Pollard. 1918.*

114

Clocks

Clocks attract attention, making them a valuable asset when a building serves as a corporate symbol. The Metropolitan Life Tower has four clocks, each 26½ feet in diameter, which face the four directions of the street grid. Behind each clock, on the 26th floor, is an immaculate little room that contains the remarkably small, original works which turn the 1,000- and 700-pound hands. The room behind the south clock is larger than the other three because it is also the company's clock repair shop. Each hour, four huge bells, one mounted on each side of the 46th floor, play what is variously called the "Cambridge Quarters" or the "Westminster Peal."

At each quarter hour, segments of the peal are heard. After 10 p.m., the chimes are silenced and a red light at the very top of the tower flashes the hour instead.

Consolidated Edison's "Tower of Light," built seventeen years after the Metropolitan Life Tower, is a half mile to its south. The tower, clock and bells are somewhat smaller, but at each quarter hour, the building sounds the same "Cambridge Quarters." To avoid interfering with Metropolitan Life's chimes, Con Ed's bells were all placed on the south side of the building, on the 32nd floor.

346 Broadway was built as the headquarters for the New York Life Insurance Company. The clocks and

eagles were added when McKim, Mead & White remodeled the building in 1899. In 1928, New York Life moved to its new headquarters on Madison Square, and subsequent owners allowed the clocks to deteriorate. Recently, however, two New York businessmen spent their spare time restoring the clocks to working order as a gift to the city. This clock is now part of the space occupied by the Clocktower Gallery of the Institute for Art and Urban Resources.

One of the loveliest clocks in the city is on the Bowery Savings Bank, and the Paramount Building was one of the last conventional (round) clocks put in Manhattan's skyline.

116 and 117

The Metropolitan Life Tower clocks at 1 Madison Avenue. Architects: Napoleon LeBrun & Sons. 1909.

Clocks *cont.*

118 *and* 119

The Con Edison Building, originally called "The Tower of Light," at 4 Irving Place. Architects: Warren & Wetmore. 1926.

120 and 121

*346 Broadway, originally
the New York Life
Insurance Company
Building.
Architect: Griffith
Thomas. 1870.
Remodeled by McKim,
Mead & White. 1899.*

THE BOWERY SAVINGS BANK.

Clocks *cont.*

123

124

The Griosic Building at
220 Fifth Avenue.
Architect: Fredrick G.
Broome. 1910.

125

The New York Life
Insurance Building at 51
Madison Avenue.
Architect: Cass Gilbert.
1928.

125

126

127

The Potter Building at
145 Nassau Street.
Architect: N.Y.
Starkweather. 1883.
The Potter Building was
the first in New York to
use terra-cotta for
exterior ornament and
the first to use it for
interior fireproofing. It is
also the oldest structural
steel building in the city.

411 Fifth Avenue
(foreground).
Architects: Mulliken &
Moeller. 1912.
10 West 40th Street.
Originally the Everett
Building.
Architects: Starrett &
Van Vleck. 1915.

128

128

The New York Times Building at 229 West 43rd Street.
Architects: Ludlow & Peabody. 1923.

129

Shepard Hall, North Campus of City College on St. Nicholas Terrace.
Architect: George B. Post. 1907.

129

Cast Iron

Cast iron was a popular material for commercial facades in Manhattan during the second half of the nineteenth century. The ornate prefabricated sections were ordered from catalogues and were much less expensive than the cut stone they imitated. Most cast-iron buildings are below 23rd Street. The increase of residential occupancy in the downtown districts of Manhattan, along with the concern of a group called "The Friends of Cast-Iron Architecture," have helped many of these buildings to be rediscovered and restored. Others, however, have been allowed to deteriorate to the point where chunks of cast iron fall to the street.

131

Haughwout Building at 488–92 Broadway. Architect: J.P. Gaynor. 1859.

130

128

WATTS STREET
PIER - 31

132
The West Side elevated
highway at Watts Street.
1930.

133

*Full-scale plane and
landing strip sculpture
on 77 Water Street.
Architects: Emery Roth
& Sons.
Designer: Rudolph
DeHarak. Sculptor:
William Tarr. 1969.*

134

134

*The Chelsea Hotel at
222 West 23rd Street.
Architects: Hubert,
Pirsson & Co. 1884.
Sarah Bernhardt and
Lillian Russell were
among the Chelsea's first
guests; later guests
included O. Henry,
Dylan Thomas and
Thomas Wolfe.*

135

*Wrought-iron gazebo
near the Con Edison
plant in the East Thirties.*

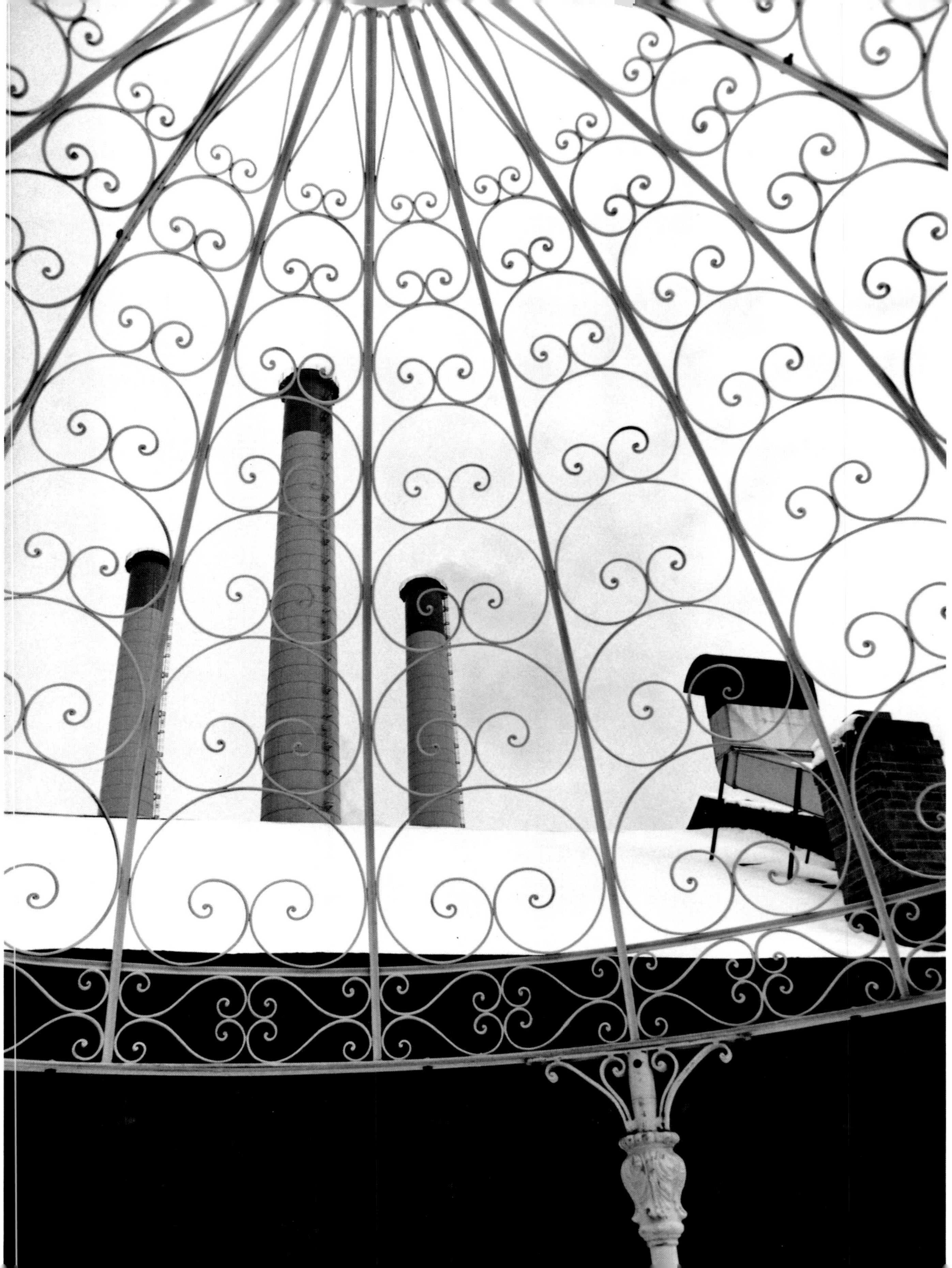

136
*Knights of Pythias
Temple at 135 West
70th Street.
Architect: Thomas
W. Lamb. 1927.
This building has
recently been
converted into
apartments.*

A Skyline Miscellany

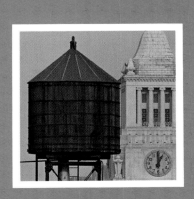

Churches, hotels and theaters are among the city's public gathering places that add a richness to the texture of the roofscape. Many of these buildings have an unusual degree of liveliness in their design to attract guests and patrons.

Before the turn of the century, churches were the city's tallest buildings and Trinity Church was the tallest of all. In 1892, a commercial structure, the Pulitzer Building, surpassed Trinity's spire, and towers of commerce have dominated the skyline ever

continued

since. Today, the surviving houses of worship seem like vulnerable little jewels whose existence is threatened by the great value of the land they sit on.

Skyscraper hotels are some of the most fanciful structures in the skyline. The 1920s and 30s not only produced the most imaginative commercial skyscrapers, but some of the most intriguing hotels such as the Waldorf-Astoria, the Sherry Netherland and the Pierre. An out-of-towner can come to Manhattan and have a fabulous skyline view from his hotel room and, as he moves about the city, find his hotel's distinctive profile from the street.

Far smaller but just as amusing are some of the city's older movie theaters, especially in districts that have been relatively unchanged since the era of fantastic motion picture palaces, which ended when World War II began. These buildings, designed to lure the pedestrian inside, have some of the most delightful facades in the city.

Another source of fascination in the skyline is created by machinery and utilitarian activities. The illusion of solitude is so prevalent in the roofscape that it is always a little surprising to see figures moving about. Yet, when one really looks, especially in good weather on weekdays, there are always people working at repairs and maintenance on building tops.

Wooden water tanks, found on most buildings that are more than six stories high, are the most intriguing of all rooftop machinery. Perhaps this is because they look so old-fashioned—they are really oversized barrels which have been made in the same manner since the last century. No one has come up with anything that works better.

Churches

137

The South Tower of the World Trade Center looms behind St. Joseph's R.C. Church at 157 Cedar Street. A line of people waiting to buy tickets to the observation deck can be seen in the South Tower lobby.

136

Churches *cont.*

138

Marble Collegiate
Reformed Church at 272
Fifth Avenue.
Architect: Samuel A.
Warner. 1854.
The Empire State
Building is visible
behind the church's
spire.

139

Saint Patrick's Cathedral
at Fifth Avenue between
50th and 51st Streets.
Architect: James
Renwick. 1858–79.

140

*Central Synagogue
(Congregation Ahawath
Chesed Shaar
Hashomayim) at 652
Lexington Avenue.
Architect: Henry
Fernbach. 1872.*

141

Saint Bartholomew's Church at Park Avenue between 50th and 51st Streets.
Architect: Bertram Goodhue. 1919.
Architects of entrance portico: McKim, Mead & White. 1902.
The portico was taken from the previous Saint Bartholomew's Church that stood at 44th Street and Madison Avenue.

Hotels

142

The Waldorf-Astoria Hotel at 301 Park Avenue.
Architects: Schultze & Weaver. 1931.
The Halloran House, originally the Shelton Hotel, at 525 Lexington Avenue.
Architect: Arthur Loomis Harmon. 1924.
The towers belong to the Waldorf-Astoria, the gargoyle to the Halloran House.

143

The Hotel Pierre at 2 East 61st Street.
Architects: Schultze & Weaver. 1929.

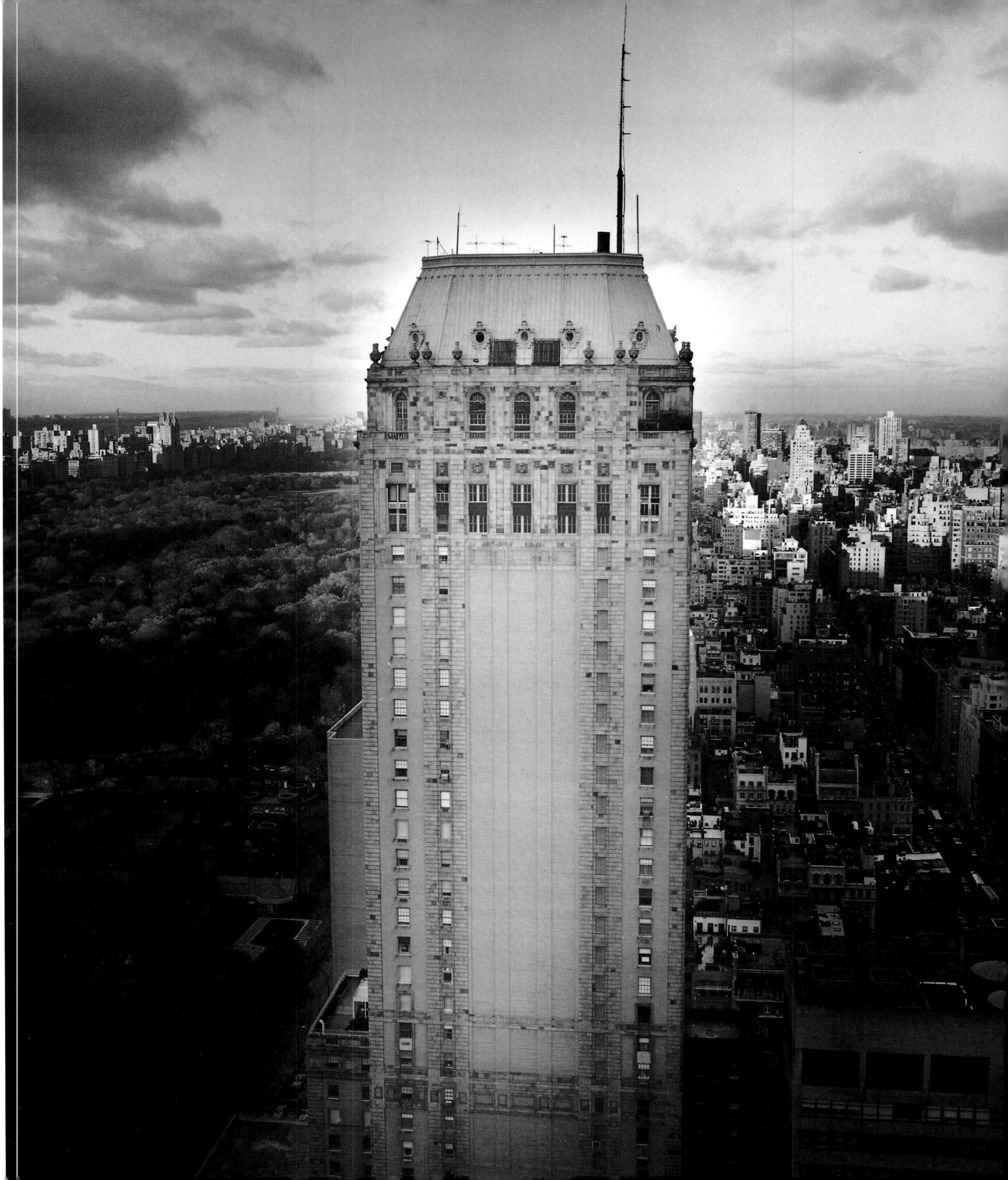

144

*The Barbizon-Plaza
Hotel at 106 Central
Park South.
Architects: Murgatroyd
& Ogden. 1930.
Calvary Baptist Church
and Salisbury Hotel at
123 West 57th Street.
Architects: Jardine, Hill
& Murdock. 1930.
The Gothic water tank
enclosure is on top of the
combined church and
apartment-hotel of the
Calvary Baptist Church.
The large building
behind it is the
Barbizon-Plaza Hotel.*

145

The St. Regis–Sheraton Hotel at 2 East 55th Street.
Architects: Trowbridge & Livingston. 1904.
St. Thomas' Church at 1 West 53rd Street.
Architects: Cram, Goodhue & Ferguson. 1914.
When these buildings were new, they were surrounded by some of New York's most fashionable mansions, and the St. Regis, at eighteen stories, was the world's tallest hotel.

Today, these two survivors are dwarfed by surrounding skyscrapers. Here St. Thomas' is seen from the roof of the hotel.

Theaters

146

3560 Broadway, originally Keith's Hamilton Theater. Architect: Thomas W. Lamb. 1913.

Upper Manhattan was a new and fashionable middle-class neighborhood during the first three decades of this century. Because this was the era of vaudeville and movie palaces, many of Manhattan's most remarkable theaters are in Harlem and Washington Heights. When I photographed the Nova Theater at Broadway between 146th and 147th Streets, I assumed that the still visible ori-ginal name, "Bunny," and the bunny faces on the facade were a logical name and motif for such a tiny, whimsical theater. A number of people who lived in that neighborhood in the twenties, however, have told me that the theater was actually named for John Bunny, an English actor known as "The Funny Fat Man" of early silent movies. For 10¢ one could see a film at the Bunny, or for 25¢ one

could go across the street and down a block to Keith's Hamilton Theater to see a vaudeville show. The Hamilton was one of the city's most lavish vaudeville houses. Today, the Nova shows mostly Spanish films and the Hamilton is divided into offices and a church. Further uptown on Broadway is the former Fox Audubon Theater (color section) which became the first theater in the district to show talkies when *The Jazz Singer* played there in 1929. A year later, Loew's 175th Street Theater opened; today it is the church of Reverend Ike. Keith's Coliseum Theater on 181st Street featured the Marx Brothers, W.C. Fields and Eddie Cantor; today it shows first-run films, but none of the original character of the interior remains. The Heights Theater shows X-rated films.

147

Nova Theater, originally the Bunny Theater, at 3589 Broadway. Architects: Strauss & Co. 1923.

Theaters *cont.*

148

The United Church at Broadway and 175th Street. Originally Loew's 175th Street Theater. Architect: Thomas W. Lamb. 1930.

149

*The Coliseum Theater,
originally Keith's
Coliseum Theater, at
Broadway and 181st
Street.
Architect: Eugene De
Rosa. 1920.*

150

*The Heights Theater at
150 Wadsworth Avenue.
Architects: Townsend,
Steinle, Haskell Inc.
1913.*

Maintenance

151

Repairs being made on the Lyceum Theater at 149 West 45th Street. Architects: Herts & Tallant. 1903.

152
Workers restoring the facing of the Woolworth Building at 233 Broadway. Architect: Cass Gilbert. 1913.

Maintenance *cont.*

Recently, when I was walking among the buildings at Rockefeller Center, a subtle movement on the surface of one of the smaller buildings caught my eye. Drawing closer, I saw that a thin sheet of water was rippling down a section of the building. Later in the day, I found that water was still flowing down the same section. Above, near the top of the building, was a cleaning rig with a row of nozzles spraying water on the Indiana limestone surface, gradually changing the familiar dark gray color of Rockefeller Center to its original golden beige. I eventually began to take photographs for the company that was doing the cleaning. To dramatize the effect of cleaning, they had a rig create the single, clean stripe through the dark left side of the RCA Building's southern facade for my photograph.

153 and 154

The RCA Building at 30 Rockefeller Plaza. Architects: Reinhard & Hofmeister; Corbett, Harrison & MacMurray; Hood & Fouilhoux. 1931–1940.

Water Tanks

157

City water pressure is not great enough to rise more than six stories, making it necessary for most taller buildings to have water tanks on their roofs. Water is pumped up to the tank and then descends to the building's faucets, toilets, sprinkler systems and stand pipes. Wood has been found to be the most economical and long-lasting material for the tanks. Since 1896, The Rosenwach Tank Company has built the largest number of wooden tanks in New York. Their tanks are constructed right on the roof in the same way as the traditional barrel. Grooved staves are loosely positioned on a metal platform and held in place with dowels. Then, ropes tightly bind the staves so that metal hoops can be placed around the tank, permanently holding it together. A conical roof is attached which contains heating coils to prevent freezing. Other companies make their tanks in factories ahead of time, and then hoist them to the roof.

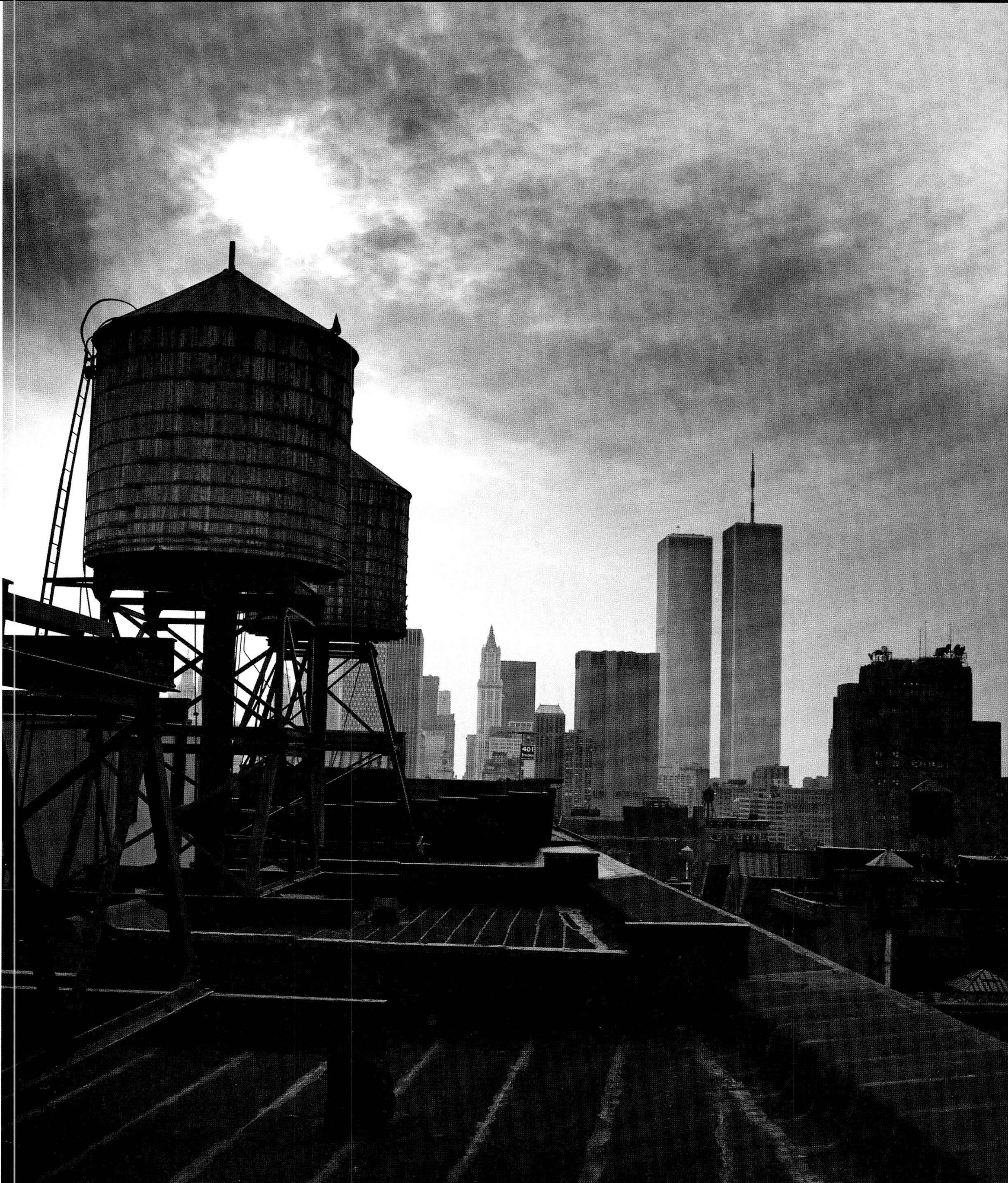

159

60 Gramercy Park North. Architect: Emery Roth. 1930.

Water Tanks *cont.*

160

*245 Fifth Avenue.
Architect: George F.
Pelham. 1927.*

*Some buildings enclose
their water tanks in
fantastic structures.*

163 and 164

Manhattan has a vast pigeon population. When the birds are not flying about or eating in the streets and parks, they sit on buildings, corroding them with their acidic droppings. Spikes are sometimes used in an effort to keep them away, as seen on the lavish carvings of Alwyn Court at 180 West 58th Street, whose architects were Harde & Short and which was completed in 1909.

163

165 and 166

*Manhattan's sky is
sometimes a place for
messages.*